Pieces and Pains of the Struggle for Justice

The source of my stories was my late grandmother
Ehrenstine Inaambepera Zauisomue

unBuried-unMarked: The unTold Namibian Story of the Genocide of 1904-1908

Contents

Prologue

In 1884, during the invasion known as the "Scramble for Africa", Germany claimed South West Africa (present-day Namibia) as her colony. Imperial Germany was looking for a living space for its inhabitants at the time, a policy better known as Lebensraum. The country sent settlers to colonize the region. As they did so, they encountered the Herero and Nama peoples, who refused to be their subjects. The German settlers started confiscating land from the Herero people and stealing their cattle. Eventually, this led to war between the Germans and the Herero, beginning in January 1904.

Germany could not easily defeat the Herero during the initial stage of the war, leading to public embarrassment for the Kaiser in Berlin. The Kaiser sent a ruthless general named Lothar von Trotha, who was also unable, at first, to put down the strong Herero resistance. Eventually, due to the Hereros' lack of ammunition and other factors, the German troops gained the upper hand and managed to defeat the Herero at the battle of Waterberg. Von Trotha was unhappy with the difficult defeat of the Herero people. He made sure to cut off their routes inland and steadily pushed them into the Kalahari Desert, where many people died of thirst, hunger and other natural calamities. The Germans later put up concentration camps for the surviving Herero and for the Nama people, who were also targeted later. The majority of the survivors died in these concentration camps.

I am the great-grandchild of survivors of the 1904-1908 Herero Genocide. This struggle has occupied much of my time for the past fifteen years. I have traveled to many European countries, including Germany, Switzerland, and the Netherlands, conducting research on this topic. I traveled to those countries because it is where most resource materials and leading academicians on the subject reside. During these travels, I have engaged in both cordial and heated conversations with diverse people about this subject. I formed friendships and made enemies as well.

I initially wanted to make a documentary film on the genocide. However, during my visits and talking to many people it occurred to me that my identity as a Namibian of Herero descent is unfortunately defined by the genocide. It is the story of my people. It is about their lost land and their struggle for justice. It is a story about my identity, that of my sisters, cousins, brothers, and other relatives with light complexion whose genes are permanently altered as a result of rape the

unBuried-unMarked: The unTold Namibian Story of the Genocide of 1904-1908

Germans inflicted on my people. Therefore, I concluded that by virtue of my identity and proximity to the story I would not be neutral Enough to give the documentary film a balanced perspective. I abandoned the project; or let me say, I decided to hold the project in abeyance.

I present here a collection of poems I wrote over the span of a few months in 2019. Each poem was inspired by an event or experience, some of which I relate here. In March of 2019, I attended a conference on the Herero and Nama Restorative Justice, which was held in Windhoek and Swakopmund, Namibia. When I visited the sites of the concentration camps and upon seeing the unmarked graves, I felt powerful and painful emotions. The campsites symbolize death, hate and human beings' capacity for immorality. And because my great-grandparents met there, the camps simultaneously symbolize love. I wondered out loud how could that be. I felt the immense energy of the desert speaking to me. And that is when the first piece titled *The Weeping Desert* came to me. About one thousand feet away from the campsites is the Atlantic Ocean. At night I could hear the waves and the cold wind singing. It must have been calling or telling me something about those who were thrown into the sea at the hands of the German soldiers in Shark Island, *The Sea Can't Swallow Me, The Bones Speak,* of our people lingering in the museums all over the world came to me as well.

These pieces were followed by *The Unlikely Friends,* a fictional account of a forged friendship of circumstances between a German camp guard and a Herero woman prisoner. I imagined this friendship because of my own experience with the Botswana police while living in refugee camps as a young man. We often shared cigarettes and beer despite our different circumstances. I was also inspired by my relationship with the white South African soldier-teachers at Okakarara High Schools during the Apartheid era. Some of them shared with us the latest Bob Marley and Peter Tosh, highly politically charged music that advocates a radical consciousness far from their own race, class and economic comfort. Our lives and conditions were separate. The soldier- teachers belonged to the class and race of the oppressor and yet there existed a relationship that helped transform my political consciousness beyond our struggle for the liberation of Namibia.

One evening after the conference in Windhoek, I was debriefing the day's discussion with a family friend, Mr. Kapombo Katjivena. As we were talking, I noticed a German-Namibian woman looking at me intensely with rage. Her rage still haunts me now. I approached her and asked, "What is your opinion about what we are talking about?" She said, "Let us step aside a little bit, I want to tell you something." As we stepped away from the group, she looked me right in my eyes and said, "You guys need to get over this genocide thing. You lost the war and that's it. We never stole the land from you. We bought the land. My great-great-grandfather bought his farm from Samuel Maharero. Stop these lies you people are telling all over the world. Get over it." I said, "You have a strong opinion about this issue. Is there a way for us to meet even tomorrow over a cup of coffee to discuss further? I would like to hear more about your perspective." She said, "There is no need to meet with me about this." And she walked away. I was stunned by her arrogance, the anger, her lack of empathy and compassion. In fact, one conference participant of Jewish descent spoke up to the German-Namibians at the conference and said, "It pains me to witness your total lack of compassion to the descendants of the 1904 genocides, and yet you feel compassion for me because I am white and Jewish." This exchange inspired me to write these pieces: *Losers and Victors, Bed Time Stories, The Past, Victors and Memorials,* and *Muherero riKarera! (Herero Stay Away!).*

During my visits to Germany, I interacted with many progressive people. However, sometimes I would make a conscious decision to step out of my comfort zone and meet those who don't think like my friends. And in most of those instances I was amazed by the ignorance of the average German person about the genocide in Namibia, let alone German colonial history. Some folks said, "I didn't know Germany had colonies. I thought it was only an English and French thing." And some said, "This was long time ago. How can you correct the past when everybody is dead?" Some people believe that successive German governments made a deliberate decision not to teach the Germans about their country's colonial past in school curriculum specifically because of the OvaHerero and Nama Genocide in Namibia. And when German people realized that indeed Germany had colonies, they become ashamed and would say things like, "How come I only learned about the Holocaust but not about the Herero genocide?" This is how the pieces titled, *No Shame, The Dead Demand Justice,* and *The Dilemma, Perplexity of Whiteness* came about.

I also met many German government officials, including ambassadors and parliamentarians. I read and heard their public statements about the genocide. My conclusion is that the majority of German leaders show very little respect, empathy or compassion with regard to the OvaHerero and Nama Genocides. In a way, I believe their racist, paternalistic view of blacks or Africans in general, have given the Germans living in Namibia a carte blanche to continue with their racist colonial mentality of superiority. Hence, the piece, *The Arrogance of Victors: Hypocrisy, Duplicity and*

unBuried-unMarked: The unTold Namibian Story of the Genocide of 1904-1908

Irresponsibility? The German ambassador in Namibia behaves as if he is a chief representing the German community in Namibia. With the exception of the former Minister of Economic Development, Heidemarie Wieczorek-Zeul, who issued an apology in 2004 at Ohamakari, for which her fellow Germans criticized her heavily. The German government has yet to pronounce itself fully on the question of the Namibian genocide.

In the case of the Namibian government, I believe that the German government uses the development aid they give to the country as a lever. The aid has impeded the Namibian government from taking any meaningful progressive stance in addressing land issues and genocide in general, because the leaders use the aid as their cash cow for personal gains. Hence, the pieces titled, *Don't Rip The Carpet Out and Conference About It But..., The Ultimate Toast with the Chancellor* and *Atrocities or Genocide?* Also, it has come to light that during the ongoing secret negotiations between the two governments about the Genocide, the German government made it clear that they are not going to refer to the events of 1904-1908 as genocide in the "legal context" but instead only in the historical context. As a result the Namibian government leaders have taken cues and do not publicly refer to it as genocide.

Of course, I could not have written these pieces if it was not for our strong Herero oral tradition of story telling. In 2004, I had the pleasure of sitting with my grandmother and asked her to tell me about the story of her parents. Where were they born? How they met and how they did survive the Genocide? She told me about her grandmother being left under a tree to die and the one of her uncle being trampled to death by the cattle stampede as they were fleeing: *Left To Die Under A Tree and unBuried-unMarked.* She told me the story how the Herero people survived in the Kalahari Desert. The cold. The hunger. The thirst. The Germans' cruelty and how they fed prisoners to the sharks in Okakoverua (Shark Island) and about her parents meeting and falling in love in the Swakopmund concentration camps. The following pieces were inspired by my grandmother's stories: *The Kalahari Diary and Treasure Found in the Namib Desert.*

As children, my siblings and I were curious about where our grandmother was born. She would say that she was born at a place called "Okatetee" somewhere in the Omaruru district about three hundred kilometers from our current village. She told us many stories about this place and her upbringing. She told us about her family journey on the wagon to the new area of the Okakarara district. She described the colors of the different oxen that were pulling the wagon and her favorite lead ox named Kambujorumbo. As children we thought this place Okatetee was just a figment of our grandmother's imagination.

In 2006, my grandmother turned 80 years old and the family held a big party for her. We asked what she wanted to do for her birthday and if there was any special place in Namibia she would like to visit. To our surprise, she said, "I would like to go visit my birthplace." We had no idea about the actual location of this place. However, she managed to describe the general vicinity and after asking around we set off. We drove to the place that was now a farm owned by an Italian family. As we were about to enter the farm, our van got stuck in the sand of the riverbed. Grandmother told everybody in the van to be quiet. She asked me get off and to scoop a piece of sand from the riverbed. I scooped a quantity of the sand about the size of two teaspoons. She grabbed my hand with the sand and licked the sand with her tongue. She spat it out and told me to do the same. She called out to our ancestors to let us in and that we had just come to visit them. She said the ancestors want us to bless the place before we entered the land. She believed that is why the van got stuck.

I got out of the van and rang a bell at the gate of the farm owner's house for help. Luckily, he was gracious enough to send a tractor to pull our van out of the riverbed. He asked, "Why are you people here anyway?" We told him this woman was born here and she wished to visit her relatives' graves and see her birthplace before she died. The farmer looked reluctant but he let us in anyway. She looked around the place and identified the sites of where different homesteads used to be and now-dilapidated graves. After we finished with our visit she said, "Now you can take me anywhere you want. I will be at peace when I die after having seen my birthplace." Hence, I wrote the piece, *The Land Is Mine.* Grandmother died three years later at the age of 83.

It would be unfair to write these pieces without mentioning the person who championed the cause when no one believed that it was one worthy of pursuing. He was ridiculed and called names for talking about genocide because the country had adopted a policy of national reconciliation. I mention the late Chief Dr. Kuaima Riruako, with whom I had the pleasure to travel in Germany. He was the first person to file a lawsuit against the German government in the U.S. His own people scorned him but he persisted. He gave me the courage to speak up and to continue capturing special moments such as the repatriation of the Herero and Nama peoples' human remains from Berlin and other important events. I dedicated these pieces to him: *Lone*

unBuried-unMarked: The unTold Namibian Story of the Genocide of 1904-1908

Bull, Ask Forgiveness, The Dead Demand Justice and *Tell The Story.*

My pieces about genocide are historical, but they are also personal and individual. They are personal in that my family and many other Namibian families went through it. They are also present and individual because of the burden these stories place on future generations. The Otjiherero language is infused with praise songs and poetry, and it emphasizes the naming of places after historical events such as the genocide. For example, in the piece entitled *The Kalahari Diary,* I referenced a place called Ozombu Zovindimba. This place is where the German troops dug wells and lured the fleeing, thirsty Herero to come drink water. As they drank the water, all of them died because the Germans put poison in the wells. My great-grandmother refused to drink from them. Hence, the place where this occurred, located in the eastern part of Namibia, was named Ozombu Zovindimba (The Poisonous Wells). Our place names, songs, and stories and the pieces in this book carry the burden of our transgenerational trauma, transmitted over successive generations of the original survivors' progeny.

The key demands of Nama and Herero peoples ar*e: A formal apology from the German parliament for the genocide committed; Germany to publicly recognize that the events of 1904-1908 were genocide; to repair the material, spiritual, cultural, and socio- economic destruction that resulted from genocide; to ensure that any reparation funds be used exclusively for the communities of people who were directly affected by the genocide; and to be able to engage directly with the German government to map out the process for Restorative Justice and the wording of the appropriate language of the apology.*

This book is about my thoughts, reflections and hopes regarding Imperial Germany's genocide of my ancestors in Namibia from 1904 to 1908. In these pages, I expose the remorselessness of the German government and society and their failure to come to terms with this ugly past. I unveil herein the psychological trauma experienced by descendants of the victims of the Genocide. This book is about aspirations, healing, resistance, restoration and reparations. It cries for justice long delayed!

unBuried-unMarked

"...my grandmother died in the war near Ozonguti. Her name was Inajovandu which means the mother of the people. She became weak and sickly during the flight toward the Kalahari (Omaheke) desert. So my grandmother's brother Kazizi and his friends instructed my mother, Maheuri, and her sister, Ngerikarere, to keep on going with the rest of the family members while they helped her and the weak."

"...In the evening Kazizi and the men rejoined the group without my grandmother. My mother asked him: 'Where is my mother?' He looked away. He told her that they had left her under a tree. 'There is nothing we could do and we are all too weak and tired to carry her.' Then my mother retorted: 'You mean you just left my mother like that to die?'"

"After this exchange my mother walked away from the rest of the family. She roamed alone in the Omaheke sandveld for some time. Then she met up with the Tjirare clan who recognized her and stayed with them until they were captured by the German patrolmen. She met her surviving family later in the concentration camps.... My mother was a fearless woman."

"...So to answer your question, my grandmother was left to die under a tree. That's the story my mother told me about her. She was left under the tree to die. She was left under the tree to die…"

Based on excerpts of the interview with my late grandmother
Ehrenstine Inaambepera Zauisomue. 2014

Figure 1. *Namibian Landscape. Etosha National Park
(Photographed by a family friend, Mr. Esmes Uaisiua)*

Tell It. The Story

wake up, wake up Uaravaera!
tell my mother's, father's and grandmother's lives
wake up, wake up Uaravaera!
i told you everything before i died
tell the story of your people

no, Grandma, i can't
i can't, i can't
i am afraid, afraid

wake up, wake up Uaravaera
tell the story of your people
tell the story of Ozombu Zovindimba
wake up, don't be crippled

wake up, wake up Uaravaera
tell the story of your people
tell the story about their bravery
their defeat and endurance

Figure 2. *Author speaking out at an anti-apartheid event.*
University of Rochester, NY. 1988. USA

Left To Die Under A Tree

let me rest under the Omumborombonga tree
my body can no longer flee
my spirit and soul will persist
will embody the spirit of generations to resist

run before they capture you
run and conquer the Kalahari desert
as they have the might to pursue
her wind, cold and your thirst remain undeterred

tell my daughters weep no more
our men fought hard but lost the war
tell my daughters to sing outjina/songs about our men's bravery
in the end they succumbed to the powerful German weaponry

run before they capture you
they have the might to pursue you
run and conquer the Kalahari desert
her wind, cold and your thirst remain undeterred

unBuried-unMarked: The unTold Namibian Story of the Genocide of 1904-1908

This excerpt from a story in an official publication for the German General Staff, *Der Kampf* [*The Struggle*] that makes explicit reference to Von Trotha's policy of extermination, even bragging about German actions:

"This bold enterprise shows up in the most brilliant light the ruthless energy of the German command in pursuing their beaten enemy. No pains, no sacrifices were spared in eliminating the last remnants of enemy resistance. Like a wounded beast the enemy was tracked down from one water-hole to the next, until finally he became the victim of his own environment. The arid Omaheke [Kalahari desert] was to complete what the German army had begun: the extermination of the Herero nation."

Mark Levene & Penny Roberts (eds.), The Massacre in History. New York and Oxford, Jan 1, 1999.

The Kalahari Diary

the scorching sun of the Kalahari
our bare feet were burning
saw mothers abandon babies
run for their safety

heard tales of grown men
forcibly suckled women's breasts for milk
it was what was left for them
the Germans even poisoned wells to kill

i refused to drink from those wells
didn't like the sight of my stomach swell
waited for the desert to decide my fate
i refused to drink from those wells of hate

saw mothers abandon babies
run for their safety
not knowing their fate in the Kalahari

heard tales of men killing loved ones
to spare them from the Germans
heard tales of soldiers playing ball
with an abandoned baby

one day the Germans must have shot Ondjembo jombepera
it was terribly cold
i dug a hole
fire would alert them of my hideout

oh, what about the old women
sickly and unable to walk
the General ordered "save your precious bullets
use dry woods and burn them"

it is strange the Kalahari could be so hot and so cold
no one ever foretold
am still angry at the man who grabbed my berries
my aching empty belly

Treasure Found in the Namib Desert

strong dark and handsome
sweat dripping down his neck
he shed no tears from sjambok whipping
many old and young men weep

cold breeze night in Swakopmund
the German guards curled in their tents
shivering and warming themselves
while I have started to like the desert moon

he stretched his scruffy hand to hold mine
his soft brown eyes shine
it's not like our place in Otjiku
it pains me when he doesn't smile

i don't want him to go
i know tomorrow he will load heavy crates onto the ship
today we scraped clean the head of the Headman
i don't understand, oh Germans
why so many skulls

i miss my mother very much, we never said goodbye
why did my uncle leave her under a tree to die
there is so much love at this camp
oh, need for sleep, today painful cramps

must tell him no sex until released to freedom
many children die in the concentration camps
our children will be dark and beautiful
will make sure to give them goat milk,
to be strong and live to carry our legacy

Figure 3. *Christian Herero women prisoners of war, captured shortly after the outbreak of war, carrying crates at the harbor in Swakopmund National Archive of Namibia*

The Unlikely Friends

for the past week he has not been the same
such a young lad of slender body frame
sitting on the rock reading the same letter everyday
i'm hesitant to ask him to kneel with me and pray

today he hasn't spoken a word
went to him and asked, what is troubling?
i can sense the sadness and see tears on his face
"meine mutter starb in Deutschland"
i put down the bag of maize

she was tall, strong and resilient
she has strong presence in the camp
i'm confused by her compassion
i lost my mother, and she has lost all

she took me to her tent and we prayed
i am surprised i stayed
no fellow German asked me of my well-being
left her tent, my grief relieved

from that day forward never saw him whip prisoners
my son about his age was trampled to death during the flight
the memory of his death haunts me to this day
i wonder what is the fate of the Herero people
they show tenacity to survive

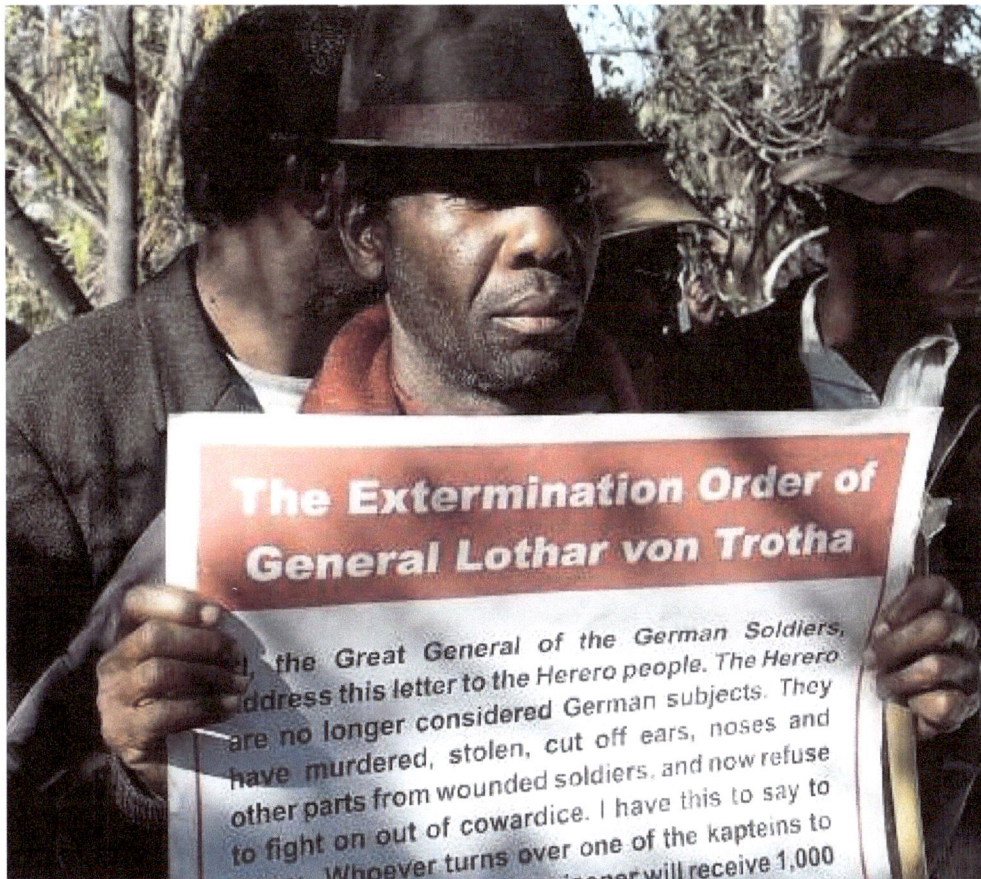

Figure 4. *Copyright of Photo: Dr. Klaus Dierks. A Herero man standing with General Lothar von Trotha's Order during the Heroes Day Memorial in Okahandja, Otjozondjupa Region. August 24, 2003. www.klausdierks.com*

Dear Gustav, Ship More

there were no good ones from the last crates
make sure the natives thoroughly clean scrape
this time send the head of a boy around eight
and a polished one of a middle-aged Herero man

life in Hamburg is same as you know
lately we've had a lot of snow
have you tried a Herero woman yet?
next week i will mail your cigarettes

Heinrich, i received yours and enjoyed it
will try my best to meet your needs
it is scary to hear the native myths
i don't like the camp superintendent's greed

haha, no Herero woman yet
one patrolman has a beautiful, well-fed one
soon his time here in German Sudwest Africa will be up
and she will be mine to try

Eine Kiste mit Hereroschädeln
wurde kürzlich von den Truppen in Deutsch-Süd-W. fl Afrika verpackt

Figure 5. *This was a postcard that was sent around 1903. It depicts skulls being placed into boxes, to be sent to the Pathology Institute in Berlin. A German solder added the following: "The skulls, which have been freed from their flesh by Herero women using glass shards, come from Hereros who have been hanged or killed in battle."*

The Bones Speak

i am not number 898
i am a victim of hate

i am not number 1512
i am a Herero you keep

let me go rest with my children
i did not come here on a pilgrimage

i am not number 3333
i want you to set me free

let me go rest with my children
i did not come here on a pilgrimage

for a century you played with my skull
and its color has become dark

a hundred plus years is enough
i am tired and fed up

let me go rest with my children
i did not come here on a pilgrimage

i am not number 2464
i am a Bushman you keep

let me go rest with my children
i did not come here on a pilgrimage

Figure 6. *Skulls of Herero, San, Damara and Nama people that were discovered at the American Museum of Natural History in New York, Personal Photo, 2017*

The Sea Can't Swallow Me

my bones resting at sea bottom
fish feast on my flesh

you thought i would be forgotten but
the salt of the sea keeps my bones fresh

the sea can't swallow me
the sea and i are one

one bright day the waves will wash my bones ashore
in my children's memory i stay

the sea can't swallow me
the sea and i are one

Figure 7. *Photographed by Jephta Nguherimo. 2017.*
Personal photo.

The Weeping Desert

take them bones
i can't bury their souls

i can no longer hide them for you
their spirits are stronger than the dunes

take them bones
i can't bury their souls

i can no longer carry the yoke of your shame
the wind and the sand speak their names

take them bones
i can't bury their souls

i can no longer hide them for you
their spirits are stronger than the dunes

Figure 8. *Unmarked Graves of the Victims of the 1904-1908 Genocide in Swakopmund, Namibia. Personal photo.*

The Lost Cow

three days in a row now
her calf is wailing in the kraal
she is the matriarch of oruzo cows
and the German wanted her to plow

if war is the means to peace
theft, rapes and hostility must cease
three days in a row now
her calf is wailing in the kraal
okutja ovita viao veuta mongaro ndjasana ngo?
(is this the manner they start their wars?)

if she is gone the whole clan will curse me
the Herero people will admonish me
okutja ovita viao veuta mongaro ndjasana ngo?
what man can't protect his women
what man can't protect his children

if war is the means to peace
theft, rapes and hostility must cease
we shall resist, fight and never bow
okutja ovita viao veuta mongaro ndjasana ngo?
they must return my cow

Figure 9. *Ongombe Jandje (My cow). Cattle are the pride of OvaHerero people. Ombuyovakuru village, Namibia. Personal photo. 2018.*

The Arrogance of Victors: Hypocrisy, Duplicity and Irresponsibility?

"...we the Germans accept our moral historic responsibility toward Namibia...but if we accept what happened in 1904-1908 as a genocide we will trivialize the Holocaust...we are ready to accept what happened in Namibia against the OvaHerero and Nama people as genocide, but reparations will not be part of such apology...then other tribes of Africa will follow suit..." "we can only give you money for projects...we don't speak to tribes, only to governments... Germany will apologize for the atrocities against the Nama and OvaHerero, but the killings were justified as they were committed in self-defense... We Germans accept our historic and moral responsibility and the guilt incurred by Germans at that time. The atrocities committed at that time would have been termed genocide ...the minister was speaking for herself... Everything I have said was an apology from the German government.." "what happened in Namibia cannot be called genocide because the term genocide was not coined at the time when the atrocities occurred"... "In particular the term genocide. We have made it very clear from the beginning that Germany does not accept a framing of the term on a legal basis; we do not see the way we will deal with history, which is 120 years old in a legal context. We have always made it clear that historic events that date back 120 years or even before World War l, cannot be dealt with on legal basis…I think we have found a lot of … how the term genocide will be used and you will see that Germany is ready to say the events of 1904-1908 represent what is called genocide, but not in a legal context."

Repeated statements I heard and read made by various German politicians and

ambassadors to Namibia

Von Trotha Extermination Order Issued in October 2, 1905

"I, the Great General of the German troops send this letter to the Herero people... The Herero people must leave the land. If they do not do this I will force them to leave with the Groot Rohr [Cannon]. Within the German borders every Herero, with or without a gun, with or without a cattle, will be shot. I will no longer accept women and children. I will drive them back to their people... "

Signed: The Great General of the Mighty Kaiser, Von Trotha

Reprinted from The Kaiser's Holocaust, Germany's Forgotten Genocide,.

Figure 10. *Newspaper clippings*

Losers And Victors

there are losers and victors
you people must stop being bitter
that's the nature and fate of history
there is no mystery
war was fought
and your people lost
get over it
your people must submit

Figure 11. *Germans at the annual commemoration of the German soldiers who died during the 1904 war against Herero people. Reprinted from Volkermord in Deutsch Sudwestafrika by Zimmerer & Zeller.*

Bedtime Stories

good night my dear, close tight the window
to keep the Herero out
always keep this under your pillow
he screams loud about his lost land

he reminisces about history
we Germans, too, felt misery
he talks about his lost wealth
he should not have rebelled

i will make sure to shut the doors
he still dreams of 1904 wars
he must accept the fate of history
and stop his quibbling

good night my dear, shut tight the window
to keep the Herero out
always keep this under your pillow
he screams about his lost land loud

his greed and imagination
far greater than other peaceful Namibians
is his thirst to avenge
keep this under your pillow for defense
for one day he will execute revenge

Figure 12. *German colonial poster.*
The caption reads "The Revenge of the Herero"
Reprinted from Volkermord in Deutsch Sudwestafrika
by Zimmerer & Zeller.

Muherero riKarera (Herero Stay Away!)

i wish you to vanish
as this land is mine now

go to Togo
go to Cameroon

as this land is mine now
i made a vow

Muherero riKarera
and let me rest

can you please vanish
your rebellion relinquished

MuHerero riKarera
and let me rest

the land belongs to me now
you stay if you become a plow

Muherero riKarera
and let me rest
can you please vanish
your rebellion relinquished

Figure 13. *The title reads "Herero You Must Stay on Your Own!"*
Reprinted from Volkermord in Deutsch Sudwestafrika
by Zimmerer & Zeller.

The Past, Victors and Memorials

tall and mighty,
guarding the spirits of those
perished in the Namib desert
breaching into the house of freedom
graves inscribed, sie gaben ihr leben fur dich
it means they gave their life for you
you must water their graves daily
and bow in their memory

Figure 14. *A controversial statue depicting German colonial soldiers' bravery. Located in front of the State House. Swakopmund, Namibia. Personal photo. 2019.*

Don't Rip The Carpet Out

don't rip the carpet
you must keep it clean
because underneath there is a casket
you must clean the stains with steam

promise do not rip the carpet
because underneath there is a hidden closet
i shall reward you with projects
and I shall not ask for progress

i command, do not rip the carpet
it keeps my dirty secret under
i command you! do not rip the carpet
i am not there to protect
i shall pay for your Mercedes
in return acquiesce to the motherland

don't rip the carpet
the bones shall be exposed
i shall reward your good deeds
with many fleets of Benz

Figure 15. *The photo represents a dark cloud hanging over Germany, in the absence of apology. Personal photo. 2016.*

The Ultimate Toast with the Chancellor

promise me and my people
that the country will be peaceful

i toast to you to confirm my faith
we will ensure the flow of aid

promise me and my people
that the Herero and Nama will not demand
as my people must keep their land
your aid will triple
if they remain civil

promise me and my people
look through the glass of champagne to see my blue eyes
i am tired of their lies
you must contain their anger and desires

promise me and my people
and the investors I will deliver

Figure 16. *Namibia's First President Dr. Sam Nujoma and the late German Chancellor Helmuth Kohl, 1995.*
Reprinted from Volkermord in Deutsch Sudwestafrika.
by Zimmerer & Zeller.

NO Shame

my story is not old
it is being told

oh, the arrogance of victors
to set the timeline
the arrogance of the killers
to set guidelines

my story is not history
it is about the burden of memory
it is about speaking up
i can't keep my mouth shut

my story is about my identity
it is about my misery
it is about dispossession
it is about liberation

my story is righteous
it is timeless
it is extraordinary
it is revolutionary

my story is not old
oh, it is being told now
it is timeless
i can't remain silent

unBuried-unMarked: The unTold Namibian Story of the Genocide of 1904-1908

"I believe that the [Ovaherero] nation as such should be annihilated, or, if this was not possible by tactical measures, have to be expelled from the country...This will be possible if the water-holes from Grootfontein to Gobabis are occupied. The constant movement of our troops will enable us to find the small groups of nation who have moved backwards and destroy them gradually."

Signed: The Great General of the Mighty Kaiser, Von Trotha

Reprinted from The Kaiser's Holocaust: Germany's Forgotten Genocide, by Olusoga &Erichsen. 2010

Conference About It. But…

conference about the lost land
and make no demands
conference about the land
and don't take a stand
conference about the lost land
but make no claim on ancestral land
conference about the land
and don't stake a claim
for your cry is in vain
conference about the land
set up a commission
and take no damn position

Figure 17. *Landscape of Namibia in Omaruru district.*
Personal photo. 2019.

Gen.o.cide.

confront your reality
and re-examine your morality
for your nation's moral fabric is broken
you can't heal without her past confronted
for your nation must repair her moral compass
to practice the morality of compassion
to practice the morality of kindness
to practice the morality of responsibility
to treat and see humanity in others

for your nation can't preach morality
because it fails to recognize genocide
because it fails to atone for the crimes
for your nation can't preach morality
because it fails to empathize

your nation must accept liabilities
your nation must seek forgiveness
in order to restore, repair her moral compass
and practice kindness and compassion
and see humanity in others
the stain of genocide is perpetual
unless and until
it is cleansed with repentance

Figure 18. *Conditions of Herero on surrender after having been driven into the desert.*
National Archive of Namibia

Atrocities or Genocide?

was it atrocities?
what word must i use *master*?
call it a national genocide?
oh, maybe atrocities?
how on earth can i name it
without offending
i am confused
i think i am being used
their spirits shall haunt me
i am confused and i plead
i think i am dreaming
i feel like screaming
what should i name it
is the state going to be legitimate?
if it doesn't advocate
oh, God am i a sinner?
you *master*! you were the killer
name it please

Figure 19. *Medal Passes the Prisoners of War in the concentration camps were forced to wear around their necks. Personal photo*

I Carried The Burden of Your Sins

she asked me to be the father
the community said it was proper
the pain you inflicted on her
will remain forever
your insatiable sexual desire
for the Herero women
fueled by your desire to break the tribe
she asked me to be the father
the community said it was proper

i am a strong man
she grew to be a strong woman
he grew to be a strong man
i am a proud father
our spirit will never be broken
the burden of your sins
i carry with no shame

Together As One

there is no need to sweat
get over the dread
sit with me at the round table
to find words that will heal my soul

words are impactful
no need to be shameful
tear down your walls of shame
no need to play a game

sit with me at the round table
and find words to extinguish the flame
the flame of bitterness
tear down your walls of shame

there is no need to sweat
let's build the walls of togetherness
sit with me at the round table
to find words that will heal my soul

Figure 20. *Waterberg Plateau, Namibia. The place where the last battle between the German Schutztruppe and Herero people took place. Personal photo. 2018*

I Am a Herero

when i speak of genocide
do not be frightened
i am not being tribal
do not tremble
i am a Namibian
my people experienced
what your people have not experienced

do not be frightened
my freedom
is your redemption
my struggle is not tribal
it is an African struggle
it is a struggle for justice

do not tremble
i am Namibian
my demands for reparations
are not tribal
it is an African struggle
rooted in justice
Europe must atone
Africa must not condone
Germany must atone
OvaHerero will not condone

i am Namibian
my demands for justice
are not tribal
it is an African struggle
do not tremble

Figure 21. *Herero prisoners hanged during 1904 -1908. National Archive of Namibia*

Figure 22. *African prisoners in chains, around 1907/1908. The man on the far left wears a pass mark around his neck.*
National Archive of Namibia

Ask Forgiveness

ask forgiveness and i will grant thee
as that will heal me
i carry the memory of my people
and i will pass it down to my children

i am from a broken tribe
and i don't want hate to thrive
ask forgiveness and i will grant thee
as that will heal me

your denial and delay
re-traumatize, resuscitate
the deep wounds of genocide
for generations i have identified

waiting for you to speak
ask forgiveness and i will grant thee
as that will heal me
only three little words

i am from a broken tribe
i don't want hate to thrive
my heart yearns for the day of your reckoning
to restore my faith in humanity

ask forgiveness and i will grant thee
as that will heal me
ask forgiveness and i will grant thee
as that will heal me

Figure 23. *Herero Prisoners of War - 1908. National Archive of Namibia*

The Dead Demand Justice

how can those who are dead still exist
and demand justice and insist
oh yeah, genocide planted the seeds
that germinate, regurgitate and strangulate

genocide silenced the voices of those defeated
the next generation sings the songs of lights
deaths planted the seeds of resistance
the lyrics of their struggle shine in lights

how can those who perished still exist
to demand restoration and repair
for that which is broken ceases
as the fruits of repair will not be fair

how can those who are dead still exist
to demand restoration and repair
the wounds are layered on the walls of the wombs
ready to shine like the moon

how can those who are dead still exist
to demand justice,
restoration and reparation
the judge must dismiss
oh no! if dismissed justice will be amiss

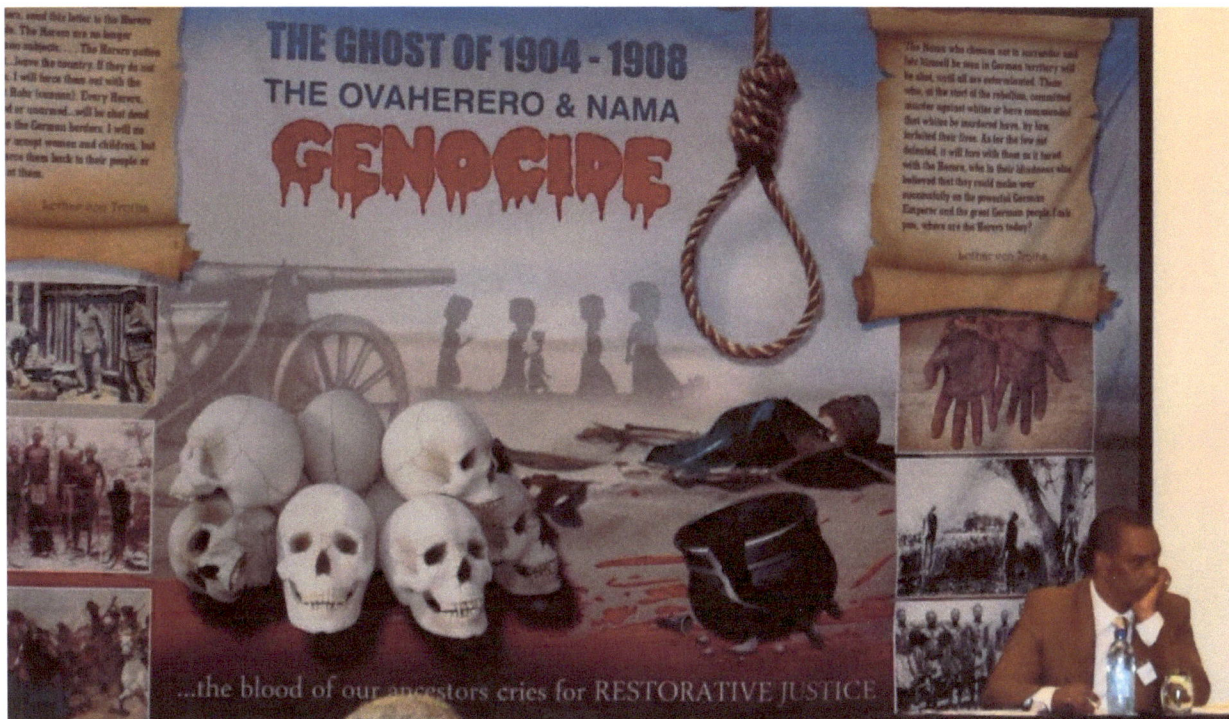

Figure 24. *A banner at the Restorative Justice Conference. Swakopmund, March 2019. On the far right corner is a Nama political activist, Bernadus Esau. Personal photo*

The Lone Bull

the lone bull died
the lone bull was tired

he took his last breath
with no fear

his sires shall carry the spear
the spear of the nation

his sires shall carry the spear
the spear of the nation

Figure 25. *The late Paramount Chief Dr. Kuaima Riruako, marching for Reparation in Swakopmund, Namibia. (Source. Unknown)*

The Land is Mine

the land is mine
i never sold you the land

the land was my shrine
the land was my livelihood

i walked it barefoot
like my cattle
and my proud ancestors before

i take a stand
i demand my land

the land is mine!
i never sold you the land

i fought for it bold and barefooted
my struggle is grounded

my struggle is grounded
like blood flowing in my veins

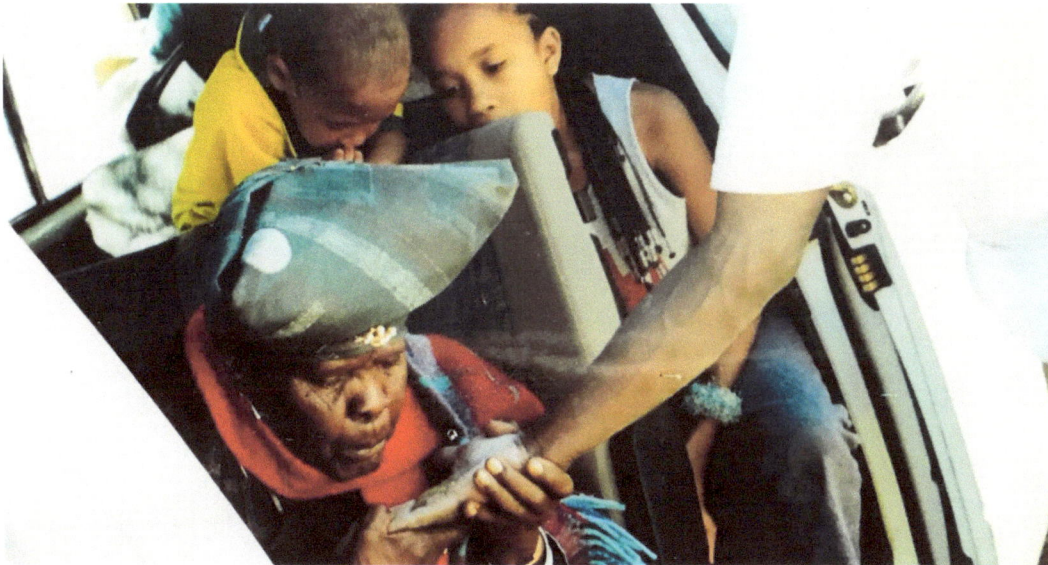

Amanda abroad
What was she doing? Looking at the picture instantly made me feel as if I can remember that day clearly. Was she blessing something? Ah I have chills 17:03

I remembering now loving she was yet, but being intimidated of her. I can picture me standing shyly behind dad and her motioning me to come over saying Tjyanduja sit down next to me, sometimes dad pushing me 😉 😅 And how powerful she talked and just listening in awe from not understanding her, but knowing

Figure 26. *Photo of my grandmother licking the sand from my hand to pay homage at ancestral land before we entered the farm, Okatetee. And the text message is a recollection of my daughter of the experience when she was eight years of age. Photo credit: Jephta Nguherimo*

Figure 27. *Sitting with my late uncle Justus Zauisomue at the holy fire discussing family matters. The holy fire is an important space where Herero people communicate to their ancestors. A place where the naming of children, healing and weddings take place. A strong cultural symbol of the people.*

The Dilemma, Perplexity of Whiteness

did i commit a crime?
oh it was in the past
they were in their prime
what to do with the memory of the past?

the noise about reparations
of the spoiled generations
my great-grandparents
why should i be burdened?
they too endured punishments

he was a merchant
fleeing religious injustice
the wages of whiteness
oh my feigned blindness

how can i restore what i've never committed?
how can i restore what my parents never admitted?
why carry the burden for what i've not committed?
how can i repair what i've never committed?

oh yeah! must i admit my privilege?
the wages of whiteness
oh yeah! the privilege of my skin tone
give me access
access...access

I Shall Be Free

one day i shall be free
and find the bones of my great-great grandmother
under the tree
one day i shall be free
to collect the bones of my people
at the bottom of the sea

one day i shall be free
and find the bones of my great-great grandmother
under the tree
one day i shall be free
to collect the bones of my people
at the bottom of the sea
and set them free

one day i shall be free
and find the bones of my ancestors
spread around the globe
one day i shall be free
and reclaim them
and set them free

Unsent Letter to my Great-Great Grandmother (Inajovandu)

your granddaughter Inaambepera,
told me your ordeal
i am still struggling to heal
i admire your bravery
angry at the Germans for their savagery

i heard they left you under a tree to die
i struggle not to cry
i pray the German soldiers did not find you
they say you were beautiful

and i heard your husband died in the battle
i am fighting for justice and carrying his mantel
the Germans deny the genocide
their souls are yet to be purified

      and while

your daughters survived the Kalahari/Omaheke sandveld
later captured and kept in concentration camps
they lived to bear beautiful children
we are not deterred, we have a vision

    With Love,

Uaravaera

References

Erichsen, C., & Olusoga, D. (2010). *The Kaiser's Holocaust: Germany's forgotten genocide and the colonial roots of Nazism*. Faber & Faber.

Förster, L. (2010). *Postkoloniale Erinnerungslandschaften: wie Deutsche und Herero in Namibia des kriegs von 1904 gedenken*. Campus Verlag.

German rules out financial reparations. (2019, June 28). *Windhoek Observer*, Retrieved from https://www.observer.com.na/index.php/national/item/11280-german-rules-out-financial-reparations

Germany returns skulls of Namibian genocide victims. (2018, 29 August). BBC, Retrieved from https://www.bbc.com/news/world-africa-45342586

Gewald, J. B. (1999). *Herero heroes: a socio-political history of the Herero of Namibia, 1890-1923*. Ohio State University Press.

Kossler, R. (2015). *Namibia and Germany: Negotiating the past*. University of Namibia Press.

Levene, M., & Roberts, P. (Eds.). (1999). *The massacre in history* (Vol. 1). Berghahn Books.

Mutua, M. (2019, July 11). To be truly remorseful, Germany should pay for Namibia genocide. *The Standard*, Retrieved from https://www.standardmedia.co.ke/article/2001333738/to-be-truly-remorseful-germany-should-pay-for-namibia-genocide

Silvester, J., & Gewald, J. B. (2003). *Words cannot be found: German colonial rule in Namibia: An annotated reprint of the 1918 Blue Book*. Brill.

Tenorio, R. (2018, August 29). Genocide of African tribes was Germany's Holocaust dress rehearsal, says scholar. *Times of Israel*, Retrieved from https://www.timesofisrael.com/genocide-of-african-tribes-was-germanys-holocaust-dress-rehearsal-says-scholar/

Zimmerer, J., Zeller, J., & Neather, E. (2008). *Genocide in German South-West Africa: The Colonial War (1904-1908) in Namibia and Its Aftermath*. Merlin Pr.

Zimmerer, J., & Zeller, J. (Eds.). (2003). *Völkermord in Deutsch-Südwestafrika: der Kolonialkrieg (1904-1908) in Namibia und seine Folgen* (Vol. 2). Ch. Links Verlag.

I would like to thank everybody who helped and encouraged me to write these collections of my thoughts. I thank my family and friends for their unwavering support. This book is dedicated to my late grandparents who raised me to be the person who I am today. My grandmother for sharing stories about the genocide, her family and my grandfather for inspiring me to fight for social justice wherever I am. I hope the pieces will provoke and inspire you to act!

Peace!!

Jephta

Pieces and Pains of the Struggle for Justice

www.ingramcontent.com/pod-product-compliance
Lightning Source LLC
Chambersburg PA
CBHW061052090426
42740CB00003B/128